For Stu Clark
and his colleagues
at the Canadian Foodgrains
Bank.

[signature]

March 2012

How to End Hunger in Times of Crises

Ignacio Trueba & Andrew MacMillan

UPM Press is the digital publishing branch of the Technical University of Madrid (UPM).

UPM Press promotes excellence in research and education through the publication of books in scientific subject matter areas covered by the Technical University of Madrid.

Catalogue

How to end hunger in times of crises

Ignacio Trueba and Andrew MacMillan / place, publisher, 2011

Number of pages Dimensions of book: 90 pages.

First edition: 2011

© of this edition: UPM Press, 2011

C/ del Pastor, No. 3 28003 Madrid.

www.upmpress.es

© of text: Ignacio Trueba and Andrew MacMillan

Editing and layout: UPM Press

Cover design: Servicio de Programas Especiales y Diseño Gráfico de la Universidad Politécnica de Madrid

ISBN 978-84-939196-1-0

Depósito legal: NA-2832/2011

Index

No Excuse for Hunger

The world has the food, knowledge and means to end hunger. Yet many people think that it is impossible. So, before we begin, let's knock 4 common excuses on the head.

1 "People are hungry because the world cannot produce enough food for all its inhabitants."
More than enough food is produced every year for all 7 billion people to eat adequately. The capacity exists to produce still more, and there is huge potential to cut back on waste and over-consumption, especially in developed countries.

The food needed annually for 1 billion hungry people to rise above the "hunger threshold" is less than 2 percent of current global cereal production, or about 15 percent of the avoidable food waste at household level in industrialised countries.

People are hungry because, although food is plentiful, they are poor and cannot afford to buy it.

2 "Famines are caused by droughts, floods and wars."
Droughts, floods and war are often the immediate causes of crop failure and livestock mortality, leading to rises in food prices and loss of income. However, even when people are starving to death, enough food is usually locally available to meet their needs, but it is hoarded by the better-off families.

Famines are man-made. With good organization, they are entirely preventable by timely actions to enable poor families to get the food that they need to survive.

3 "People are hungry because they are lazy and don't want to work."
Chronically hungry people simply do not have the energy to work or study, and so have no capacity to earn money to buy food. They are caught in a trap from which escape by their own means alone is virtually impossible.

The first step towards eradicating hunger must be to ensure that all under-nourished people have the means to acquire the extra food that they need for a healthy life.

4 "Giving poor families grants to buy food creates dependencies and undermines their dignity."
Can any condition of life induce greater dependence than being constantly denied access to adequate food? It deprives people of all opportunities for betterment, and exposes them to frequent illness and premature death. It is like preventing people from having medicine when they are sick.

A well-functioning society makes sure that all its members can eat. Everyone, rich and poor, stands to benefit from greater prosperity and peace.

Many people living today will have to eat in 2050.

About this Book

In 2006, Ignacio Trueba published a book entitled *The End of Hunger in 2025 – A Challenge for our Generation*. We are now updating this material, drawing on lessons that we have learnt over the past 5 years, and setting it in the context of the serious crises that have hit the world during this period. We are also extending its focus to address the goal of how to feed the world's population in 2050. We examine how this can be done sustainably and in the face of the added problems posed by the processes of climate change.

Given the diversity of the intended readership, the book is published in two versions – a more comprehensive professional version, available as an e-book, and a short version for people who want to end hunger, which is available both in printed form and as an e-book. Interested readers of either version can refer to the website **www.endofhunger2025.com** for additional data, graphics and background papers.

This is the *short version.*

Our aim is to awaken public opinion to the scale and nature of the hunger problem and to the fact that it can be quite readily solved in a permanent and sustainable manner. We demand that governments and the responsible international bodies make a true commitment to address the horrifying situation that, in our world of plenty, one in seven people should still suffer from chronic hunger.

Our book is addressed to people who are involved in policy-making and in taking decisions. But it is also written for all people who care about the hunger problem, especially those involved in civil society movements, whose support is of vital importance if governments are to be persuaded to take the hunger problem seriously.

All royalties from the sale of this book will be donated to the Got Matar Community Development Group for use in their educational programmes. See: www.gotmatar.org

School children at Got Matar, Kenya

Thanks

The authors wish to express their thanks to the present Director-General of FAO, Jacques Diouf, for writing the Foreword, as well as to José Graziano da Silva, who has recently been elected as FAO's next Director-General for the period 2012-15, for his Observations at the beginning of the book.

We also want express our sincere gratitude to a group of experts, professional colleagues and researchers who prepared short background papers within their areas of specialisation, that served as a valuable source of ideas and information on which we drew in writing this book. Their names are listed on the inside leaf of the back cover, and their papers can be accessed, together with additional data, on the website **www.endofhunger2025.com**

We wish to give special thanks to Beatriz Pecker, Ana Afonso and Monica Tarancón for their commitment to this work and for all that they have done to make its production possible. We want to highlight their exceptional professional competence, enthusiasm, organizational capacity, sense of responsibility and unlimited patience! We also wish to thank Marta Pedrajas, Francisco Bueno and Elena Trueba for their valuable comments on the Spanish drafts, as well as Percy Bono, Patricia Tendi, Kate Singleton, and Tom and Rebecca MacMillan on the English drafts.

At the same time we wish to express our profound thanks to Fernando Pizarro, an international irrigation expert, fine professional and good friend, who died recently and worked closely with us in the writing of this book.

Finally, we offer our profound thanks to the Technical University of Madrid (UPM), the UPM General Foundation, its Higher Technical School for Agronomists, and the College of Agronomists of the Central Region for their professional and financial contributions that have made this work possible.

Works in an irrigation channel in Peru. (Fernando Pizarro)

Foreword by
Jacques Diouf,
Director-General of FAO

Almost 10 years have passed since FAO put forward the concept of a twin-track approach to combating world hunger. It called for combining improvements to the productivity and incomes of small-scale farmers through strategic investments with ensuring access of the poor to adequate food, mainly through social protection programmes. While these approaches remain valid, their application has been made all the more difficult by the recent crises that have swept the world, and particularly by extreme volatility in food prices.

One consequence of this price volatility was that the number of hungry rose sharply between 2006 and 2009 to reach a peak of 1,020 billion, after which it dropped, partly as a result of the incipient global economic recovery. However, FAO finds that hunger on any scale is unacceptable in a world that has the capacity to feed all its people. Of particular concern is the condition of people living in protracted food crises: FAO has identified 22 countries in which hunger is a recurrent or persistent feature of many people's lives.

FAO recognizes that world leaders are faced with an exceedingly challenging food security environment, but still believes that it is entirely possible to feed all 9 billion people expected to be living in the world in 2050 if the right policies are applied. A reaffirmation of the Declaration of Human Rights, particularly the Right to Food, must now top the global political agenda. A global dialogue on the international governance and coordination arrangements of food related issues is essential and urgent. World leaders must also increasingly acknowledge the role of an emerging civil society that supports a value system based on coexistence, equality, justice, peace and human development.

Finally, I wish to express my gratitude to Ignacio Trueba and Andrew MacMillan for making the case for rapid hunger eradication and for shifting to truly sustainable food production systems.

Observations by

José Graziano da Silva,

FAO Director-General Elect

The rise in food prices in 2006-08 and the financial-economic crisis of 2008-09 made it clear that the old recipes for addressing hunger and extreme poverty no longer work. The combination of a prolonged fall in investment in agriculture, of the political decision to reduce strategic food reserves, and of the increasing dependence on the international market proved to be fatal. According to FAO, between 2008 and 2009, the number of hungry people in the world rose from 923 million to 1,020 million.

Now, in 2011, a fresh rise in the prices of foodstuffs is happening that again threatens the food security of millions of people. The repetition of a food crisis within a period of just 30 months confirms what FAO already signaled a couple of years ago: food price levels would continue at higher levels than those that prevailed before the 2006 crisis and there would be an increase in price volatility.

To guarantee global food security requires a fundamental revision of the global agricultural system and a new international consensus which is both translated into effective action and backed by the necessary investment of financial resources.

I am delighted that, in this little book, my friends Ignacio and Andrew have addressed the same themes that were central to my successful bid to become Director-General of FAO. I called for the rapid eradication of hunger, the creation of a truly sustainable equilibrium between food consumption and production, and greater fairness in the way in which global food systems operate. These are issues of fundamental importance to humanity, which we must address together with renewed commitment and vigour.

Chapter 1
End Hunger Now or Let it Continue?
A Choice for All of Us

The most fundamental ingredients of life are air, food and water. Most of us take all three for granted. Indeed, many people have now come to regard other things as also vital for a normal life, such as decent clothes and housing, and perhaps even a car and a mobile phone.

But this is not the daily reality for all.

Over the past 30 years, the economic policies pursued by governments have led people to buy 600 million cars and 5 billion mobile phones, but they have also created conditions in which 800 to1,000 million humans remain deprived of sufficient food and of safe water supplies. The sheer size of these figures is numbing. What they really mean is difficult to grasp, unless we try to think what hunger in our own family – literally not knowing where the next meal will come from – would mean to us, our parents and our children, and then to all our friends and their families, and so on, until we reach a thousand million people.

For some people, having their car or mobile phone stolen

seems like the end of the world. But, when it comes to chronic hunger, millions of people are literally having a chunk of their life stolen from them each day.

Why, we must ask, do we turn a blind eye to a human tragedy being played out on such a massive scale around the world?

That millions die prematurely each year because of chronic hunger, in a world that now produces enough food for all people to eat adequately, and that has the skills and resources to send men to the moon, defies logical and moral explanation. It seems to be a result of ignorance, apathy, greed, upside-down priorities or incompetence. Sometimes hunger results from deliberate action – or inaction - by governments and international bodies.

Maybe we have to look at the lack of concern about hunger as a by-product of the processes of "development" to which all nations that aspire to modernity subscribe, and in which most of us are caught up in our daily lives. Perhaps hunger is the ultimate manifestation of a progressive breakdown in the caring or compassionate dimension of human behaviour. Or maybe it is the ugly face of what we claim to be modern civilization. We could also think of it as the consequence of allowing unfettered greed to hijack the promises of a better life for all, offered by the processes of globalization and modern means of communication.

When governments were faced with a financial crisis, they rushed to commit billions of dollars to bail out banks when these came close to collapse through their own mistakes, claiming that they were 'too big to fail'. When there was a food crisis, however, governments turned down the proposal that they should commit themselves to eradicating hunger by 2025, in spite of evidence that the goal was feasible. Perhaps, for those who wield the power to rescue banks, the hungry, in spite of their numbers, are simply 'too insignificant to matter'.

Whatever the reason for lack of serious action, the result is *famicide* on a vast scale: by this, we mean killing off those who are hungry through a failure to act to prevent their predictable premature death. It is quite as horrific as genocide, but it is not recognized as a crime, and nobody is brought to justice for it.

This famicide is all the more terrible because eradicating hunger is now entirely possible and does not cost very much, compared to all the other things on which the world is spending money.

Indeed, all countries have promised, over and over again, to reduce hunger, but few have acted with deliberate intent. This may be partly because there is little effective pressure from their people to do so. However, if you ask anyone in any country if they would wish another person to be hungry or to starve, almost all would say "No". But the idea that this implies - that it is morally unacceptable that one in seven humans should be chronically hungry - is not reflected in the extent of popular indignation that one might expect. Perhaps we have been anaesthetized by the bewildering mix of huge numbers and jargon, so often used to explain the problem. Despite, or perhaps because of, the images we repeatedly see of emaciated men, women and children, we seem unable to connect with the suffering of even one child. Is it because, as Marc Zuckerberg, the founder of Facebook, said: "A squirrel dying in front of your house may be more relevant to your interests now than people dying in Africa"?

Maybe we do not know that there are proven and affordable solutions that, if applied, will bring huge benefits not just for the hungry but for all humanity.

Another reason for inaction is the common view that ending hunger is impossible because the world simply cannot produce enough food to do it. The truth is that, at least for now, there is ample food for everyone to eat adequately. Annual food waste at consumer level in industrialised countries (222 million tons) is almost as high as total net food production in Africa (230 million tons)[1]. To close the gap between what 1 billion hungry people are eating now and what they need to consume to climb above the hunger threshold would require the equivalent of only 25 to 30 million tons of grain per year or just over 1 percent of the 2.3 billion tons of grain now being produced. Even if the amount needed was to be doubled, or even tripled, and its food content diversified, it would still be insignificant in global terms. It is not a big deal!

The main stress being placed on available food supplies comes not from the hungry but from all of us who are wasting good food and eating much more than we need, and often damaging our health in the process. Yet most of us are not aware how our lifestyle choices affect the lives of those who produce our food, and how they damage the environment.

As more people understand the hunger problem and call for action, governments will hopefully be compelled to take it seriously. And so this book provides the key facts and explains the main issues, against the backdrop of the five man-made crises – food, climate change, energy, environmental as well as economic and financial – that now face the world. It claims that hunger and the ways in which food is produced, traded and consumed have fuelled these crises, and suggests that ending hunger and adjusting the ways in which food is grown and eaten can play a key role in preventing their recurrence and in contributing to peace.

Food plays a central role in everyone's lives, to the extent that what and how much a person eats has a fundamental impact on their quality of life and well-being - their health, how long they live, whether they can learn well at school and can get a good job. We now see extreme divergences in what people eat, with both extremes facing ill health, whether from being hungry or from over-consuming food. This should be worrying for governments, not just for the health and livelihoods of individuals – but because it also has huge human rights, economic and environmental implications.

The concept of the right to food has its roots in the Universal Declaration of Human Rights and in the International Covenant for Economic, Social and Cultural Rights, that has been ratified by 160 countries. A United Nations general comment on the latter states that "the right to adequate food is realized when every man, woman and child, alone or in community with others, has the physical and economic access at all times to adequate food or means for its procurement[ll] ".

People who are hungry are effectively denied the right to adequate food. But they are also excluded, through their weakness and consequent lack of income, from contributing to the growth and development of their countries and from playing their full role in society. This not only holds back development but, as we have seen recently in Tunisia, Egypt, Syria, Yemen and other countries, becomes a huge source of frustration that spills over into unrest and violence.

The production and consumption of food also has major environmental impacts, and is one of the main sources of greenhouse gas (GHG) emissions that drive the processes of climate change.

Amazing advances in technology and the unrelenting quest for prosperity are pushing the processes of globalization ahead at breakneck speed, much faster than our ability to harness them for the general good of humanity. The challenge is not to slow these processes – that would be impossible – but to take the fullest possible advantage of them to bring about improvements in nutrition and in the production of food.

A strategy to free humanity now and for ever from hunger

must focus on two main objectives.

The first goal is to eradicate hunger as fast as is humanly possible. Because the usual cause of hunger is that those people who most need food cannot afford it, the core action must be to provide quite modest but regular grants to families to enable them to bridge the gap between what they are now eating and their basic food needs. This requires no new knowledge, but simply good organization as well as funding. The necessary investment will quickly pay for itself.

The second goal is to create a truly sustainable basis for meeting all future global food needs: this will require some new knowledge and lots of inspired and creative thinking. However, there are already good precedents on which to build programmes.

In the following pages, we will provide you first with some facts and figures about hunger and the food management system. We shall then show how food production and consumption are linked to the various crises that have struck the world over the past 5 years. Subsequently, we shall suggest how to approach the goals of ending hunger and shifting to sustainable consumption and production patterns. In the final chapters, we will draw some conclusions and suggest some initial actions that could usefully be taken now at national and global levels.

Our message throughout is that each of us, whatever we may do in life, can play a part in inducing the required changes. If we succeed, the world will be a better, fairer and safer place for all its people, now and in the future.

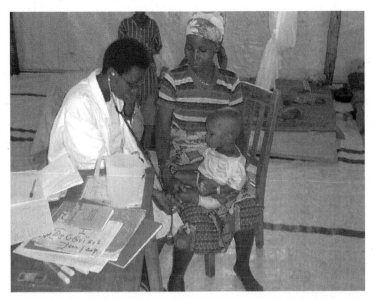

Good mother and child nutrition assures a healthy future.

Education is critical for a country's development.

Labour-intensive rural road construction provides a strong motive for community participation in development.

Farmer Field Schools increase local decision-making capacities.

Chapter 2
Hunger

When people are said to be suffering from hunger, it is because they are not eating enough food to enable them to lead a fully productive and healthy life.

Hunger may be *acute*, as in times of seasonal shortages, drought or war. *Famine* is the most extreme manifestation of acute hunger: it results in people starving to death. Famines occur even where adequate supplies of food exist (often hoarded by better-off people) simply because many people have used up all their reserves and so have no means of acquiring it[III].

Chronic hunger is a condition of life in which people are habitually under-nourished. Long-term lack of adequate food intake usually has serious impacts on both the physical and mental growth of children and on the working ability and intellectual capacity of adults. Many people who are hungry suffer not only from a shortage of energy but also of protein, essential minerals and vitamins. Such deficiencies raise their susceptibility to disease and to premature death.

The term *malnutrition* is usually used to refer to the combination of a deficient diet and related illness. It can also be used in relation to over - or unbalanced - consumption of food, that often leads to obesity and related diseases, including diabetes, heart diseases and dementia.

Measuring What People Eat

To understand the scale and nature of the hunger problem, measurements of food availability and consumption are needed. One of the simplest approaches is to add up all the food available in a country – from annual production plus imports minus exports, adjusted for changes in stocks – and divide this by the total number of inhabitants. When the different food types are assessed according to their energy content and divided by 365, this results in an estimate of mean *Dietary Energy Supply* (DES), expressed in kilocalories (kcal) per person per day: note, however, that DES is a useful indicator of hunger but fails to pick up other aspects of malnutrition. DES varies greatly between regions. Thus, at the end of the 20th century, the world average DES was 2,803 kcal/day, with industrialised countries averaging 3,380 kcal/day and developing countries 2,681 kcal/day: in sub-Saharan Africa, the mean DES was 2,195 kcal per day[IV]. Recent figures show that ten countries in Africa, as well as Haiti, have DES levels of below 2,000 kcal/days[V].

DES, however, covers both the consumption and waste of available food. In some developed countries, 30-40% of available food is wasted. Much less is wasted by households in developing countries, and in many cities food wasted by the rich is scavenged by the extreme poor: however, losses in storage and distribution are big, mainly because of poor infrastructure. Actual *Food Intake* after these losses is measured through household surveys.

To survive, everyone needs a certain basic energy level to keep the body alive. This amount is known as the *Basic Metabolic Rate* (BMR), and varies according to a person's sex, age, weight and height. The Food and Agriculture Organization of the United Nations (FAO) estimates that adults in developing countries need a minimum food intake of between 1,720 and 1,960 kcal/day for basal activity and light work (usually calculated as BMR multiplied by 1.2). Thus a person with a BMR of 1,500 kcal/day needs 1,800 kcal/day to be lightly active. In sum, anyone eating less than 120 percent of their estimated BMR is classified as hungry[VI].

How much food energy individuals require, over and above this amount, depends on their level of activity (i.e. how much energy they use). Manual workers may require an energy intake of 190 percent of their BMR (or, for our example, 2,850 kcal/day). A person who eats this amount every day but who is not using up the energy through exercise is almost certain to put on weight.

Conversely, the amount of work that someone can undertake is determined by the amount of their food energy intake above their BMR requirements. Hungry people do not have the energy to work hard and are therefore unemployable and unable to earn money. They are caught in the "hunger trap" from which escape through their own means alone is almost impossible.

Facts and Figures

Since the end of the Second World War (WWII) in 1945, the earth's population has grown from 2.5 billion to 7 billion. Food availability per person has risen, on average, by 40 percent. In 2009, global production of cereals was about 2.3 billion tons, and meat and egg output about 325 million tons.

In spite of this, almost 1 billion – or one in seven – of the world's population are chronically hungry. About 3 billion more suffer from various forms of malnutrition, including from vitamin and mineral deficiencies. Some 1.5 billion people are overweight or obese. The implication is that well over half the world's people do not eat healthily.

Millions of people die prematurely each year because of causes related to both under-nutrition and obesity. The number of people dying each day from hunger-related causes is thought to be about the same as the rhythm of death during WWII (24,000 per day). About two thirds of those now dying of hunger are children[VII].

Chronic hunger as well as malnutrition, caused especially by shortages of protein, vitamin A, iodine and iron, impair both physical and mental development. Thus, if children are born underweight or have inadequate nutrition when very young, they will never be able to grow and learn to their full potential. Nutritionists claim that the period between a child's conception and second birthday - their first 1,000 days - provides the best window of opportunity for interventions to address hunger and malnutrition[VIII].

More than twice as many hungry people live in Asia (578 million) as in Africa (239 million). There are more hungry people in India (251 million) than in all of Africa. However, the proportion of people who are hungry is higher in Africa (30 percent)[IX]. According to the World Food Programme, hunger is found in all countries, but 65 percent of the hungry are in just 7 countries – India, China, Democratic Republic of Congo, Bangladesh, Indonesia, Pakistan and Ethiopia.

The number of people who are chronically hungry is very sensitive to the international price of food. FAO's Food Price Index (100 in 2002-04) remained relatively stable from 1990 to 2007 but then more than doubled to almost 220 in June 2008, averaged 157 in 2009, and rose to 232 in May 2011[X]. These big changes in food prices have occurred even though there has continued to be enough food in the world for everyone.

International trade in food has grown rapidly, with food exports estimated to value over US$1,100 billion in 2007. The trade is dominated by a few corporations, giving "the food commodity chain an hour-glass shape in which millions of producers sell to billions of consumers through a very narrow join made up quite often by only four to eight firms"[xi].

Several of these firms also dominate the agricultural input supply market, especially for seeds, pesticides and fertilizers. This means that they exert huge power in relation to the world's food supply and how it is distributed.

Poor families spend about 70 percent of their income on food, compared to about 10-15 percent spent on food by high and middle-earning consumers. The food consumed by poorer families tends to be of lower nutritional quality. When prices rise, poor people have no alternative but to cut their already low consumption, while the better-off continue to eat as they normally do or cut back on some luxury food items.

Most people are hungry because, although there is sufficient food grown and in the market, they do not have the means with which to buy their families' food needs or are unable to produce enough through their own efforts. Some are hungry because of natural disasters or war. Some 70 percent of the hungry live in rural areas. Most of these are small-scale farmers who sell some of their production but who do not earn enough to buy their other food needs. Many, however, are very small-scale subsistence farmers and landless people. Many of the urban hungry are migrants from rural deprivation.

Population growth, along with rising incomes, is one of the sources of increasing demand for food. Annual world population growth fell from a peak of 2.2 percent in 1963 to 1.1 percent in 2009, and is predicted to continue to fall. Even with falling birth rates, however, total population will rise from 7 billion now to about 9 billion in 2050, partly because people are living longer. Global population will probably stabilise at around 9.5 billion in the latter half of this century[XII], when fertility levels reach replacement rate (an average of 2 children per couple)[XIII].

About 1.5 billion hectares (13 percent of the world's land area) are used for farming. About 80 percent of the farmed area is used for rainfed agriculture and 20 percent is irrigated. Around 40 percent of all food output is from irrigated areas, which have doubled over the last 50 years. Between 1961 and 2008, the area of cultivated land per person has shrunk from 0.44 ha to 0.25 ha.

Rainfed agriculture uses 4.5 percent of the world's renewable fresh water resources, and a further 2 percent is used for irrigation. About 3,000 litres of water are used in producing the food consumed each day by each person on earth. About 70 percent of fresh water used by humans is extracted for irrigation. Because fresh water resources are very unevenly distributed, however, some areas enjoy ample availabilities, whereas others (Near East/North Africa, South Asia) are facing severe constraints.

What people eat and waste has a major impact on GHG emission levels and on the pressure exerted on water and land resources. The environmental impact is now commonly expressed in terms of one's *ecological footprint* that summarises the impact not just of one's food use but also of other demands on natural resources, including transport, heating etc. Eating a kilogram of grain-fed beef has more than twice the footprint than the same amount of pork or chicken, and 15 times that of 1 kg of bread[XIV].

A mixed diet is nececessary if people are to enjoy their right to adequate food

Food plays a vital role in our lives.

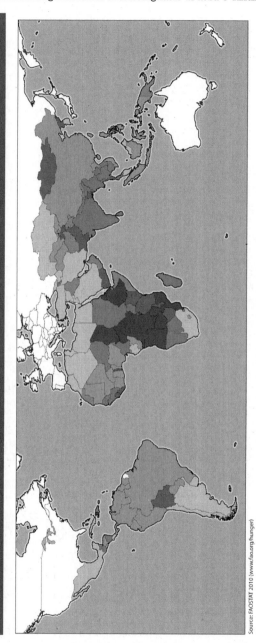

Source: FAOSTAT 2010 (www.fao.org/hunger)

FAO Hunger Map 2010
Prevalence of undernourishment in developing countries

Prevalence of undernourishment in developing countries (2005-07)

- Very high (undernourishment 35% and above)
- High (undernourishment 25-34%)
- Moderately high (undernourishment 15-24%)
- Moderately low (undernourishment 5-14%)
- Very low (undernourishment below 5%)
- Missing or insufficient data

Undernutrition by Region

Asia and the Pacific: 578 million	62%
Sub-Saharan Africa: 239 million	26%
Latin America and the Caribbean: 53 million	6%
North Africa and Near East: 37 million	6%
Developed Countries: 18 million	2%

Chapter 3
Food and the Global Crises

For the past 5 years, the world has been rocked by severe crises, and they are not over yet. Food and oil prices rose to record levels in 2008-09, and food prices are on the rise again in 2011. Severe weaknesses in the financial and banking systems, combined with high and volatile commodity prices and shifts in exchange rates, have triggered disastrous economic performance in the major industrialised economies. This led businesses to close, imports to plunge and unemployment to rise.

Throughout the world, the brunt of these crises has fallen, however, on those who are least able to cope – the poor and hungry – swelling their numbers and prompting severe social unrest, armed conflict and migration.

Governments are belatedly waking up to the need for far-reaching changes in the way their economies run, in order to reduce their impact on the environment, and, especially, to make drastic cuts in the GHG emissions that drive the processes of climate change.

This combination of inter-related crises threatens the quality of life, wellbeing and peaceful coexistence of the 7 billion of us who now live together on this planet – and it is bound also to profoundly affect the lives of future generations.

The biggest mistake that we can make is to address these crises, as it now the case, separately. To see how they can be resolved, it is essential to examine, from a multidisciplinary perspective, the issues that underlie the crises. This is particularly so when we consider options for eradicating hunger and for changing the ways in which food is produced, traded and consumed, so as to create a sustainable equilibrium between food supplies and human needs.

We view the crises largely as a consequence of our generation's incompetent, irresponsible and greedy management of the world's human and natural resources. The world has allowed itself to be driven by the untamed quest for economic growth. Governments – and society at large - have chosen to turn a blind eye to the disastrous impact that this can have on the poor as well as to the dangers of exhausting the natural resources that our children will need for their survival. We, therefore, agree with assertion by José Graziano da Silva of "the need to tie the processes of economic growth much more tightly to greater social inclusion – and this means that we have to rethink the type of development that we are looking for"[XV].

The crises are a wake-up call for nations, singularly and collectively, to move quickly away from policies that tend to promote an ever-growing level of consumption of goods - including policies that implicitly promote over-consumption of food - to more responsible approaches to growth and globalization that are shaped by due respect for the fundamental concepts of fairness and sustainability and respect for human rights, including the right to food.

We fear that, if we do not react to the current crises responsibly, they will lead, as they did in the Great Depression of the 1930s, to greater political turbulence, further economic and social instability, an unravelling of global institutions, and, eventually, to conflict on a scale that will undo all the progress made since the end of WWII – when the United Nations was founded as part of a vision of a world in which there is universal "freedom from want".

The processes of development and globalization cannot be turned around overnight. There is, however, no better place to start to show how they could work more equitably, in the interests of all humanity and of future generations, than to get to grips with hunger eradication and the future supply of food.

We will, therefore, explore the linkages between the global crises and food production and consumption. We will then suggest how, through exploiting potential synergies, ending hunger and feeding the world's future population can be done in such ways that they become part of the solution to the current crises rather than a cause.

The Energy Crises

Our food is produced mainly by the process of photosynthesis, through which sunlight converts water and nutrients, absorbed from the soil by the roots of crops, into plant growth. Plants may, in turn, be fed to farm animals for conversion into meat, milk, eggs and other foods. Only about 2 percent of energy absorbed by plants is transformed by crops into food, and only 11 percent of the energy in crops fed to livestock emerges as edible products.

Modern intensive food production systems are high users of energy of fossil fuel origin. This is used by farm machinery, such as tractors, combine harvesters and pumps. Fertilizers and pesticides have high fossil fuel contents, and additional energy is used in transporting, processing, packaging and cooking foods for people to eat. About 20 to 30 percent of the cost of bringing food to the table is due to energy costs, making the cost of producing food highly sensitive to changes in crude oil and natural gas prices.

For a variety of reasons, oil prices rose by over 5 times between 2003 and 2008 when they peaked at US$146 per barrel. Such energy price instability – which contributes to and is reflected in global food price volatility – accentuates the already very big risks and uncertainties to which farmers are exposed. The growing concern over the finite nature of oil and gas resources seems bound to lead to higher energy prices in future, implying that food prices will also have to rise, at least so long as food is so fossil fuel dependent.

Many industrial countries have provided large subsidies for producing so-called "first generation" bioethanol and biodiesel, made from human foods, including maize, sugar, soya and palm oil. In 2007, this diverted about 100 million tons of grain into biofuel production. This contributed to scarcities, especially of maize, that further pushed up international grain prices.

One of the big challenges for agriculture is to reduce its heavy dependence on fossil fuel and hence buffer its sensitivity to fuel prices while also cutting GHG emissions.

Environmental Crises

Climate Change. Most governments now accept that, since the beginning of the industrial revolution, human activity has been inducing a process of climate change that is accelerating. The consensus is that the driving force is the release of GHG into the atmosphere, causing a rise in average atmospheric and oceanic temperatures, which will change rainfall patterns, making some areas drier and others more humid, with huge implications for food production.

Currently, climate change is driven mainly by developed countries which, with 15 percent of the world's population, generate 45 percent of global GHG emissions. Some 11 percent of the world's population live in Sub-Saharan Africa but create only 2 percent of total emissions. The effects, however, are felt by all countries[xiv].

Agriculture accounts for about 15 percent of total global emissions, and deforestation, usually to make way for farming, for a further 11 percent. This means that producing our food is one of the major drivers of climate change. At the same time, farmers, because they are so dependent on the weather, are also amongst the most vulnerable to changing weather patterns. Indeed, climate change will be one of the main threats to future global food security.

GHG emissions are usually measured by the amount of carbon dioxide (CO_2) equivalent released into the atmosphere. The *carbon footprint* of food varies enormously, depending on how and where it is produced. So what we eat makes a big difference to the extent of noxious emissions from agriculture. A high energy/high protein diet, typical of industrialised countries, has a carbon footprint that is 3 times as high as that of a better balanced but healthy diet.

Land and Water At the global level, land availability is not a constraint to raising food production in the foreseeable future. It is estimated that a further 2.8 billion hectares (almost twice the area now farmed) are potentially suitable for rainfed cultivation. Much of this "spare" land is in Sub-Saharan Africa and Latin America, and a large part is under forest or savannah vegetation. Great care, therefore, must be taken in converting any such ecologically rich or fragile lands into additional farmland and, indeed, they are probably best not used for farming except under extreme food emergencies or through using agro-forestry-based cultivation systems. Worryingly, almost all suitable land is under cultivation in densely populated South Asia as well as in the arid Near East and North Africa, and the situation is quite tight in the rest of Asia.

From a hunger eradication perspective, water is vital for both human consumption and food production. Many of the families that suffer from hunger, especially those in rural areas, also lack access to clean water and sanitation, further raising their susceptibility to disease.

Fresh water accounts for only about 1 percent of the earth's total water resources, most of which are saline. It is in the same two regions in which there are land shortages – South Asia and the Near East - that fresh water scarcity has begun to limit water available for agriculture, including for expanding irrigated areas. Here, agriculture is increasingly competing for available water with industrial and human consumers, both of which are able to pay more highly for their supplies. The implication is that, unless low-cost systems for desalinating sea water are developed, increases in locally produced food supplies will have to come from higher water use efficiency and higher yields per unit of water consumed[XVII].

To the extent that there are local and regional scarcities of both land and water, these are being exacerbated by various processes of degradation, usually caused by poor land management, high-intensity farming and industrial pollution. Any such damage to finite land and water resources, as well as the conversion of prime farm lands to urban and industrial use, is particularly serious because it is not always reversible and so limits options for their future utilisation.

Removal of forest cover and frequent tillage cause erosion and increase sedimentation in river beds, making them more prone to flooding. The spread of cultivation onto marginal areas leads to desertification. Irrigation systems, built without adequate drainage, as has often been the case, become subject to salination. High levels of fertilizer use tend to pollute surface waters with phosphorous and groundwater with nitrates. Pesticides, especially when they are used in conjunction with irrigation, are also leached into groundwater, as are nitrates from feedlots and aquaculture. This is an insidious process, taking many years, but ultimately one that risks making previously safe water supplies undrinkable and a source of illness. The overall cost of damage caused by nitrogen release, much of it from agriculture, has recently been estimated at US$100-450 billion per year in Europe alone[XVIII].

Biodiversity. Concern over threats to the integrity of the world's biological diversity led countries to create a Convention on Biological Diversity in 1993. Much has been achieved since then to conserve important ecosystems. Paradoxically, however, the greatest threats to biodiversity come from the processes of agricultural intensification which narrow the range of crop and animal species and varieties on which our food production depends, because, understandably, farmers tend to replace lower yielding with higher yielding varieties. Large-scale monocropping systems and related reductions in the organic matter content of soils that result from frequent tillage greatly reduce the extent of biological activity within farming systems and diminish their resilience to pests and diseases. Yet the importance of maintaining genetic resources for future use in plant and animal breeding is greater than ever, in view of the need for farming systems to adapt to the impacts of climate change.

The Economic and Financial Crises

The economic-cum-financial crisis has had some surprising impacts on agriculture and food consumption. One might have expected that, at a time when global food supply seemed to be more or less in balance with demand, food prices would have fallen in response to a drop in consumer spending. Instead, however, they rose sharply for four seemingly disconnected reasons.

First, although many of those involved in the international food trade deny that excessive financial "speculation" pushed up food prices, the effect of higher food costs was for millions of poor people to become hungrier, because the pittance that they could afford to spend on food bought still less of it[XIX].

The second factor that raised food prices was the combination of a spike in oil prices, and of generous subsidies on biofuel production in Europe and the USA. This reduced the availability of grains and oilseeds for human consumption.

Third, some analysts claim that rising demand for grain to be fed to livestock to respond to growing meat demand, triggered by rises in incomes in India and China, put additional strain on the international cereals market.

Finally, there is a perception that global food stocks have been narrowing, which is probably correct. However it is difficult to prove because the private companies that are involved in food commodity trading are not required to disclose their stocks and they treat the information as a trade secret.

Whether these explanations are correct on not, however, may not matter too much. What is clear is that the results of the financial and economic crises and of the accompanying extreme volatility in food prices have been devastating for low income consumers and small-scale farmers alike.

Between 1969-71 and 2005-07, the number of hungry people in the world hovered between 800 and 850 million - but this jumped by about a quarter to 1,023 million in 2008-9 because of the sharp rise in global food prices[XX]. Once low-income consumers shed assets in order to pay for food, as is the case when hunger strikes, it makes it almost impossible for them to emerge from deep poverty. The situation of the poor in many developing countries has been further worsened by big drops in remittances, especially from migrant workers in the USA and Europe, that started to decline in late 2008 in response to rising unemployment[XXI].

Even in normal times, farmers are exposed to many risks, especially those caused by weather, pests and diseases, with the result that they think twice before investing in expanding production. High food prices, if passed on to producers, could be expected to have made them decide to expand output, but the price volatility of 2007-2009 seriously dented farmers' confidence in the markets for their products.

A further side-effect of peak food prices is that several food-importing developed and emerging economies have started to buy or lease land in Africa and Latin America for growing part of their future food needs. This contentious process has moved faster than the capacity of the countries involved to establish policies and regulations to limit potential negative impacts. There is special concern about the damage to indigenous communities that might already depend for their livelihoods on the lands that have been allocated to investors by their governments, often without any prior consultation or compensation[XXII].

Sowing in Senegal.

Water Is essential for life.

Chapter 4
Two Big Challenges for Humanity

Many people are so overcome by the effects of these crises that they think that we are crazy to call for an end to hunger at this difficult time. We believe, however, that serious flaws in the way in which food is managed are fuelling all the above crises, though, of course, they are not their only cause. This leads us to think that progress in reducing hunger and malnutrition, and putting food production, trading and consumption on a sustainable footing, are critical elements in resolving all the current crises and preventing their repetition.

The first challenge is to make sure that all humans have enough food to eat as soon as is possible. It is imperative to address the injustice that, when the world can feed all its people, around 1 billion chronically hungry people still face ill health, shortened lives and total exclusion from all the pleasures that so many of us take for granted. It is very important to enable young children to eat well because, if they are malnourished in their earliest years, they will never be able to recover their full potential. We call on all countries to aim to end hunger – once and for ever – by 2025 or even earlier if possible.

The second challenge is to bring about a shift towards a sustainable equilibrium between food production and consumption. If human life is to continue on earth in the long term, it is essential that our future food needs be reliably supplied by truly sustainable means of production. The sooner we make the transition to sustainable production systems, the better. To make this task easier, however, there is a need to moderate future growth in food demand. We cannot, on ethical grounds, go on expanding food output to respond mainly to a demand that is driven by consumption levels that are far above dietary needs, when this destroys the very resources on which future food supplies have to depend. Nor is it acceptable to prolong a situation in which many of the farmers, forest dwellers and fishermen, who produce our food, remain amongst the poorest and most deprived people on earth. We believe that, if the right steps are taken as of now, a sustainable balance between production and consumption of food can readily be attained by 2050.

It is helpful to look at these two challenges separately because, although they are inter-connected, the measures required to address them and the key players involved are distinct.

Ending Hunger by 2025

Surely the most fundamental responsibility of any government is to run its nation in such a way that its citizens are able to eat adequately. It seems self-evident that a government that pursues policies that deny any of its people access to the food that they need to live in health is failing in its most basic responsibility towards its people and going against its commitment to their human right to adequate food.

In an increasingly globalised situation, we believe that it must also be a collective responsibility of all nations, but especially those that have benefited most from market liberalisation, to ensure that all people can eat well. Every nation, therefore, has obligations to ensure that global food management systems are run fairly and equitably for this purpose[XXIII].

In Box 1, we look at how one country – Brazil – has successfully tackled its hunger problem.

BOX 1
Brazil's Zero Hunger Programme

Zero Hunger, launched by President Lula in 2003, has confirmed that, with firm political commitment, popular support and visionary leadership, fast and lasting progress can be made in cutting hunger through programmes that simultaneously broaden access to food and stimulate small-scale farm production. A main lesson is that the use of targeted social protection programmes that provide quite small but regular grants to the poorest families, combined with universal school meals, can bring about rapid hunger reduction and, at the same time, trigger a range of other good social and economic outcomes: income distribution has improved, with incomes of low earners rising over 5 times as fast as top earners; the number of people living in poverty fell by 24 million; labour force participation rose faster amongst programme participants than non-participants; the mortality and stunting rates amongst under-5 year old children dropped significantly; and school attendance and learning performance has improved. In addition, with over 90% of the monthly cash transfers, paid to 12 million poor families, being allocated through adult women, the status of women in the home and in society rose sharply. The programme also protected poor people from the impact of the recent global crises. Finally, much of the funding for the programme's social protection components has ended up as increased income for small-scale farmers who have supplied the extra demand for food. All this has been achieved at a cost of around 0.5% of GDP [xxiv].

Brazil's success strengthens our confidence that the immediate problems of hunger and malnutrition can be overcome by 2025, or even before then, if more countries address hunger frontally, rather than through the use of indirect measures. Our conviction is also based on the following considerations:

• A number of other developing countries (e.g. Armenia, China, Congo, Ghana, Jamaica, Mali, Myanmar, Nigeria and Vietnam) have already met the Millennium Development Goal (MDG) of halving hunger by 2015 and others are well on the way, showing how it can be done: all of these countries have given high priority to measures to improve food access for the poor.

• The most difficult aspect has already been solved. Every year, even at the time of the recent food price crisis, more than enough food is being produced to meet much more than the dietary requirements of the world's population.

• The incremental amount of food required to close the hunger gap is, as we have noted, very small in relation to present global food output and the volume traded, provided that measures to improve food access are accurately targeted on those most in need.

• Big gaps exist between the potential crop and livestock yields, as shown by researchers, and those now generally achieved by farmers: this yield gap can be narrowed even without heavy new investment.

• Global communications and trade systems are adept at matching food availability with demand: if the food *needs* of the hungry can be translated into *demand*, the market will respond, except perhaps in very remote or war-torn areas.

• Massive over-consumption and waste of food can be curbed: apart from reducing the pressure to increase food output, this would lead to huge health benefits and significant GHG reductions.

• Subsidies on bioethanol production from maize and other grains that produce relatively low net energy benefits can be cut.

• The costs of ensuring that everyone is able to eat well are miniscule in relation to the huge size of the global economy and to government spending on less vital matters including the weapons of war.

• The benefits of ending hunger will be felt by us all:

　　• Within concerned countries, the most blatant injustices will be ended, erasing needless tensions that can erupt in violence: there will be big falls in child mortality, a surge in the size and fitness of the labour force, better attendance at school and enhanced learning abilities, longer life expectancy and reduced health costs, and much greater human resilience to natural disasters and other shocks.

　　• At the global level, there will be a lower risk of conflict and of political, social and economic instability, and migratory flows will drop.

Shifting to Sustainable Food Production and Consumption Systems by 2050

Unfortunately, a large part of current food output comes from farming and fishing practices that are damaging the natural resources and rural societies that are needed eventually for growing food for a population expected to rise to 9 billion by 2050.

The major sources of damage include:

• Expansion of the farming frontier into unsuitable areas and fragile ecosystems.

• Frequent use of ploughing and other cultivation methods that invert soil and thereby degrade soil structure, release stored carbon into the atmosphere, limit retention of water and reduce fertility, leaving soils prone to erosion.

• Localised over-extraction of fresh water resources, their pollution, especially by pesticide and fertilizer residues, and salt build-up on poorly drained irrigated lands.

• The accelerating spread of crop and livestock diseases, including, in some cases, their transmission to humans.

• Reductions in natural biodiversity and narrowing of the genetic basis of the main food crop and livestock species.

• Contributions to climate change processes through high GHG emissions from intensively managed crops and livestock.

• To these must be added, over-exploitation of many of the ocean's fish stocks, infringements of animal welfare, the encroachment of buildings onto good farm land, and the frequent exploitation of human labour at all levels within the food system.

One reason for using destructive production methods has been that most governments have adopted food policies that have the implicit goal of keeping prices low for consumers. This has been good news for low-income urban households but tragic for rural producers. More seriously, it has the side-effect of subsidizing middle- and high-income households, providing incentives for over-consumption and large-scale food waste. These low food prices have only been possible because the costs of environmental and social damage have been ignored and not paid, whether by producers or consumers. Many of the current crises stem from these policies, which have also led to gross under-investment in farm assets, rural infrastructure, and agricultural research because the financial and economic returns have been relatively unattractive.

Our confidence that it is entirely possible to move to a sustainable equilibrium between food consumption and production in the coming years, and even before 2050, is based on the following grounds:

• Even if the 70% growth in food demand in 2050, forecast by FAO, was to materiliaze, this could be met by rates of food output expansion that are lower than those attained recently.

• The FAO demand forecast assumes that, as their personal incomes rise, most people will, as is now happening, make the transition to the high calorie/high protein diets adopted by "western" consumers and follow similar patterns of food wastage. It also assumes the continuation of current population growth trends. There is good scope, however, for moderating future demand growth by promoting healthier and less environmentally damaging diets, cutting waste and slowing future population growth.. Our estimates suggest that such measures could reduce the level of extra production required by 2050 to about 50 percent above current levels[XXV].

• Many farmers in developing countries are already switching to more sustainable food production systems that produce high yields with lower use of fossil fuel based inputs, and they are increasing their incomes in the process[XXVI]: this trend will be boosted by expected increases in oil prices and by rewarding farmers for reduced GHG emissions.

• Agricultural research programmes, if properly funded, can avail themselves of existing infrastructure and staff, on which to begin rebuilding their capacities. Even though government extension systems have collapsed in most developing countries, many valuable experiences in farmer education and empowerment exist and can be widely emulated.

• The main directions of technology change towards sustainable agriculture and those for cutting greenhouse gas emissions coincide and are mutually reinforcing.

As disposable incomes rise and poor families get better access to school and health services, birth rates come down, and this trend can be accelerated by providing access to reproductive health care services. Lower birth rates will certainly help to cut poverty. However, their net impact on food demand would be quite limited as reductions in family size would be largely offset by increases in per caput consumption within the family. A large part of the forecast population is, in fact, the result of the longer life expectancy of people who are already alive.

Chapter 5
Conclusions

Our starting point has been that food is a vital ingredient of life. Yet, as we have seen, the ways in which its production, trade, marketing and consumption are being managed are deeply flawed and unjust. In this chapter we begin by briefly listing the main problems. We then explore possible strategies to address them at national and global levels to achieve rapid hunger eradication and to make the required shift to sustainable food consumption and production systems.

Deep Flaws in Food Management

The main problems can be summarised as follows:
• Too much of our present food production comes from using farming and fishing methods that irreversibly damage the fragile and scarce natural resources needed to provide food for future generations: these methods also contribute significantly to climate change processes.

- No safeguards are in place to ensure that global food security is not unduly exposed to risks of future shortages, or to prevent excessive short-term price volatility that undermines production incentives and can quickly throw more people into extreme poverty and hunger.
- Food commodity trading, farm input supplies, food processing and food retailing are largely in the hands of a relatively small number of international corporations who are driven by profit motives and are not required to disclose information. This seems incompatible with the global public interest of ensuring the adequacy of global food supplies, including stocks. It could also be an impediment to a shift to more sustainable production systems that are less dependent on purchased inputs and hence likely to be resisted by the big companies that shape producer and consumer behaviour in many countries.
- No international body has the power to intervene to ensure that, if serious global shortages should occur, the burden of coping with them would be shared equitably and not fall, as now, on the poorest, raising levels of premature death, while the rest of us continue to eat all that we want.
- Policies that keep food prices low for all consumers encourage excessive consumption and waste by the majority of the world's population, threatening their health and exacerbating environmental damage: they also undermine incentives for investing in agricultural research and in expanding food production, using sustainable farming methods.
- Moreover, low food prices fail both to compensate for environmental damage caused by food production and to improve living conditions for food producers. Low prices leave the most vulnerable amongst producers in an endless cycle of despair and uncertainty, with all the attendant psychological and physical tolls.
- The hunger problem is man-made[XXVII]. Although natural

disasters, conflict and food price spikes increase the risk of people being exposed to food shortages, outbreaks of acute hunger and famine can be prevented by timely action on an adequate scale. Chronic hunger is mainly the result of global and national economic policies that have fostered economic growth in ways that have accentuated income disparities. Almost 1 billion people are hungry, condemned to ill health, premature death and exclusion from the mainstream of society, not because of lack of available food but because they cannot afford to buy it or are otherwise denied access to it. This is not only morally unacceptable but also economically short-sighted.

• Flaws in the food management system have played a central role in triggering the food, energy, economic/financial, environmental and political crises that have recently hit the world. The persistence of hunger and malnutrition will continue to have destabilizing effects, until resolved.

• So far, the response, in the area of food management, to these crises, both at international and national levels, has been unconvincing. It has been driven more by short-term national, sectoral and commercial interests rather than by a genuine commitment to make the world a better home for all its people, in which everyone can enjoy their right to adequate food.

• Over and over again, governments have committed themselves to cut the incidence of hunger, but few have translated their words into action. Those that have done so, show that rapid progress is possible and that huge health, economic and social benefits can stem from this.

• Other governments may have tried to end hunger but have achieved little because they have applied the wrong strategies. They have often sought to solve the problem mainly by raising food output - which may be necessary to meet rising demand but does not necessarily help the hungry. Most governments have tended to avoid options for curbing overconsumption and for providing those who are hungry with the means to buy or produce the food that they need.

• Donor governments have consistently failed to deliver on their funding commitments and have opposed the idea of adopting a time-bound goal for hunger eradication.

• One reason for lack of government action is that there is little vocal public support for ending hunger and malnutrition, and still less for reducing excess food consumption and waste. Perhaps this can be partly explained by the fact that the public has never been provided with all the facts – including the fact that there are quite simple and affordable solutions.

• This lack of apparent public outrage is unjustifiable, given the huge scale of human suffering and lost potential that is caused by chronic hunger. Hopefully this can be changed by harnessing the power of modern communications to expose the immensity of the problem in *real time*, and to build a consensus that this injustice – this "*famicide*" - must be quickly ended.

Changing National Strategies

We are convinced that the world can feed all its people, now and in the future, but that this will require fundamental changes in mainstream thinking on the problem, followed by appropriate action.

First, we must reiterate that a very clear distinction has to be made between the goals of ending hunger and malnutrition on the one hand, and of placing the food security of nations and of the world on a sustainable footing, on the other. Achieving each of these goals requires different sets of actions. Yet the two goals are inter-related and have to be addressed through coherent policies and effective institutions that span both sets of issues at global, regional and national levels. Success in ending hunger by 2025 will be an important milestone on the road to sustainable food security by 2050.

On ending hunger and malnutrition, we recommend that all governments give the highest priority to launching direct measures that will bring about quick results in terms of improved nutrition among the poorest members of society. This means giving top priority to ensuring that all currently undernourished people have the means to either buy or produce at least the extra amount and quality of food that they require to live healthily. For this, we advise governments to put in place nation-wide targeted social protection programmes, that provide regular monthly grants to poor families to allow them, at the very least, to attain food consumption levels that enable them to escape from the hunger trap. Box 2 says more about the justification for this proposal.

BOX 2
Ending Hunger - Getting Priorities Right

Even a young child knows that the best cure for hunger is a square meal. Most people who are hungry cannot have a square meal simply because they are too poor to buy the required food.

Strangely, few governments have addressed the problem directly. Many try to maximize economic growth and to expand food production, hoping that this will end the hunger problem, as the benefits trickle down to the poor. FAO's projections show that when such policies are pursued, there will still be 370 million hungry people in the world in 2050, even if average global food output per person increases by over 35 percent.

A steady increase in food production to meet expanding global food needs is necessary. However, except when the extra output comes from families that are themselves facing hunger, it will have little immediate impact on the number of hungry. The big breakthrough can only come in the short term through providing income transfers to very poor families to enable them to purchase their basic food needs. When well targeted and administered, these programmes enable families to improve their food intake - the best, cheapest and only medicine for hunger – and hence put them in a position to escape from the hunger trap. Unlike food aid, such grants stimulate local markets and allow recipients to choose the food that best meets their needs. In the longer term, approaches to national economic growth that assure more equitable sharing of the benefits offer the most sustainable solution.

Direct measures to reducing hunger, however, still invite much criticism, in spite of the fact that many countries are adopting them. Critics say they are "unaffordable", "unsustainable" and "create dependency" – but can any condition induce more dependence and destroy human dignity faster than that of a mother not knowing when her children will next eat? And how can a country reasonably aspire to "development" as long as a quarter or a third of its population is excluded by their hunger from being part of the process? Aiming for development in such situations without addressing hunger is like trying to drive a car with one foot on the accelerator and the other on the brake!

Given that the average depth of hunger per under-nourished person is about 250 to 300 kcal per day [XXVIII], transfers equivalent in value to around just 70 grams of cereals per day (or 25 to 30 kg per person per year) would be sufficient to lift a typical individual out of hunger (i.e. to raise food intake to 120 percent of BMR). The cost would be about US$2.50 per month per family member (an amount that needs to be indexed to local food prices and adjusted accordingly in order to assure effective protection when it is most badly needed, should prices rise). In countries that can afford more, there would be advantages in aiming for higher allowances as this would speed up the rate at which families would emerge from deep poverty and be able to stand on their own feet.

Such a minimalist social protection programme, based on a regularly updated register of eligible families, would provide a foundation onto which other relevant activities can be progressively added in line with resource availability, growth in institutional capacity and, above all, the response capacities of the beneficiaries. Priorities would respond to locally identified needs and opportunities for improving nutrition, health and food availability, with the aim of enabling people to graduate quickly from dependence on social protection. Such additional activities could include:

• Nutrition education and food supplementation, targeted on mothers and on their children under 2 years of age.

• Enabling small-scale producers, especially those subsistence farmers and landless rural people who benefit from social protection, to improve their capacity to feed their families from home-grown food.

• Redistributing idle farm land to food-insecure families.

• Skills training to enhance participants' employment opportunities.

• School meals and complementary school gardens programmes.

- Community-led infrastructure improvements, especially for clean water and sanitation, but also rural roads to provide better links to services and markets.
- Better access to primary health care, including reproductive health services, as well as education, especially for girls.

Fundamental to all of this is a progressive build-up of skills and capacities at the level of local government and within communities, as well as in households, both rural and urban. One approach to empowering people living in rural areas to improve their farming systems and to cope better with the many issues that threaten their livelihoods is to enable them to take part in Farmer Field Schools, described in Box 3.

BOX 3
Farmer Field Schools

The idea that a field could be a school arose in Java in Indonesia in 1989 when farmers found their rice crops being devastated by a pest called the Brown Plant Hopper. Usually, in the early days of the Green Revolution, when pests appeared, farmers were encouraged to spray more insecticides. The odd thing about the Brown Plant Hopper was that the more they sprayed, the worse the attack became. The reason was that spraying killed off the Hopper's natural enemies that had kept it under control in the past. Simply telling farmers to stop spraying did not work either, as they did not believe what they were told would help. So the idea arose that, if farmers saw with their own eyes that there were good and bad bugs in a rice field, and observed their life-cycles and how they interacted with each other, and how broad spectrum insecticides killed the good ones, they would be able to devise and apply practical control strategies. About 25 to 30 farmers would come together with a facilitator once a week during the crop season and divide up into 4 smaller groups to observe the health of the rice plants and identify the problems: each group would then report back to the others on their findings, and, collectively, they would decide what actions to take. Often farmers would set up experiments to test alternative strategies. One common action taken to control the Hopper was to remove the egg masses manually from the young rice seedlings at the nursery stage. Farmers started to apply the same approach to other problems that they faced.

This was the beginning of the Farmer Field School (FFS) movement which has spread all around the world, empowering millions of farmers to take responsibility for addressing many diverse issues – whether to do with crop and livestock production, erosion control, marketing, coping with AIDS, food security etc.

Usually a new FFS group is provided with a start-up grant to pay for the services of a facilitator (who may be an agricultural extension officer but is often a farmer who has graduated from a FFS), for teaching materials and some inputs. The proceeds from sale of products from the study field or enterprise are retained and used to finance the next year's study programme, perhaps on a different topic of local relevance[xxix].

To sum up, we see social protection not as charity or "welfare" but as an economically sound investment that, beyond correcting gross injustices, will generate large economic benefits where these are most needed, in poor communities. Solving the food problems of the poor ends their isolation and enables them to participate in the labour market, to begin investing in productive assets and to become consumers in their own right. It provides an excellent entry point for further actions to address other constraints faced by the poor, because, until people are adequately fed, they are in no condition to be able to respond to other initiatives.

What we are advocating implies a fundamental shift from supply-driven to demand-driven approaches to addressing hunger. The resources provided through social protection have the combined effect of improving the health of people to a point at which they can escape through their own efforts from the hunger trap, while, at the same time, creating a new market for goods and services, including food. This, in turn, can stimulate agricultural growth, especially by small-scale farmers.

In parallel with this, we see the need for a *green evolution*, aimed at putting food consumption and production on a sustainable basis. This means simultaneously curbing growth in excessive food use and waste, and creating conditions for expanding food production to match expected demand (including the amount resulting from social protection). The rise in food output, however, must be achieved while shifting towards truly sustainable production systems.

To curb growth in excessive demand for food, we propose that governments of countries in which a high proportion of the population is consuming more food than needed for a healthy life adopt strategies that have the aims of progressively slowing the rate of population growth, reducing the extent of over-consumption of food, cutting food waste, and eliminating subsidies on biofuels made from food and feeds. Deliberate efforts to adjust each of these parameters, even quite modestly, to cut future demand could, as a consequence of synergy, lead to a reduction in incremental food demand in 2050 from the forecast 70 percent to about 50 percent or even less. This would result in healthier and more equitable food consumption patterns and lower environmental stress.

In almost every country, including those in which there is widespread hunger, there are good opportunities as well as precedents for increasing local food production. This extra production should, wherever possible, come from small-scale rather than industrial farmers because the multiplier effects are much greater in terms of employment and income distribution, as explained in Box 4. We see the rise in food output coming initially from closing the large gaps between the yields that farmers are currently achieving and those attained by researchers under similar ecological conditions. This will require limited public investment in services and infrastructure. The next stage, that of making the transition to sustainable production systems, implies a great broadening of farmers' engagement in participative extension and adaptive research, aimed at improving their ability to make informed decisions on how best to use their labour, land and water resources as well as livestock. It will also call for increased investment in improvements in rural infrastructure, especially irrigation and drainage schemes as well as roads.

Throughout these processes, we should not forget or dismiss farmers' own sources of knowledge and their remarkable resilience to shocks, factors that have allowed them 0to adapt to changing environments for generations. One example of such knowledge relates to the planting of appropriate trees in arid zones. Trees not only provide soil protection, mitigate climate change by combating desertification, and maintain biodiversity, but they are also important providers of human and animal food, fuel, shelter and sustainable livelihoods, particularly for women.

BOX 4
Small-scale Farmers can Meet Most
of the World's Additional Food Needs

There is much debate on the respective roles of small-scale and large-scale farmers in feeding the world. It is clear that both have important parts to play. However, the more that the extra food demand can be met by small-scale farmers, the greater will be the social and environmental benefits. Many developing countries in which agriculture depends mainly on small-scale farmers, have successfully increased output to keep pace with fast rising demand.

The expected growth in food demand offers one of the best opportunities for economic betterment in rural communities. If the extra production comes from big, heavily mechanized farms, few people will benefit and the owners (who may not live in rural areas or even within the same country) will seldom invest in improving local conditions of living. In contrast, if it comes from small-scale farms, it can generate lots of employment opportunities and the extra income will be shared by many more people. The mixed farming systems used by most small-scale farmers protect biodiversity and complex ecologies. Being less dependent on machinery and on fossil fuel based fertilizers and pesticides, food produced by small-scale farmers has a relatively low negative impact on climate change processes, ecological stability and water quality. Small-scale farms can also make good use of many of the marginal land areas which are unsuitable for heavily mechanised systems.

Throughout the developing world, small-scale farmers continue to be the main suppliers of food consumed by the local population, producing an estimated 80 percent of all food marketed in Africa and Asia. They have been the main contributors to the growth in agricultural production in developing countries which, at 3.7 to 4 percent per year, has been more than twice as fast as output growth in industrialised countries since the 1970s. They have also shown great capacities for innovation.

Their continued role in expanding food supplies, however, is threatened by the neglect of rural areas by many governments and by an unjustified perception within some governments that only large-scale input-intensive farming systems can meet future demand. There has been a long period of under-investment in research and extension activities to respond to small farmers' needs; in water supply and sanitation; in rural roads and electrification; in reliable and renewable sources of energy and access to credit; in education and health services, and in opening up land ownership options for landless rural people. All of this, combined with low producer prices for food, has led to a situation in which poverty and hunger are heavily concentrated in rural communities, and to a massive wave of migration to the cities, swelling their slums.

And so, a very important part of the move towards greater sustainability of food production is to create conditions in which small-scale farmers can see tangible incentives for staying in rural areas and hence better respond with increased production to rising food demand. Essentially this is a matter of allowing human capacities within rural societies to flourish by working with them to analyze the problems and opportunities that they face, and to help them organize themselves to address them. Apart from providing them with opportunities to learn about and test technologies that can meet the rising quality requirements of expanding markets, it means encouraging them to strengthen their bargaining position in the market, for instance through raising their confidence to come together in associations or cooperatives. But it also calls for creating a much improved technical and management capacity at local level to respond with know-how, financial support and information technology to the aspirations of rural communities for better infrastructure and services. Moreover, it requires policies that recognize and compensate small-scale farmers for the important environmental and ecological services that they provide.

The main longer-term challenge is, therefore, to develop and encourage farmers to take up practices that do not damage the environment; are more resilient to climate change and other shocks, and result in higher yields and improved incomes. Fortunately there are good technical precedents, already being applied on a very large scale in many parts of the world, for increasingly sustainable ways of producing food. These include, for example, various agro-forestry systems, integrated crop/livestock systems, organic farming, multi-storey cropping, conservation agriculture/ zero tillage, and sustainable rice intensification (see Box 5). All of these systems harness natural processes to enhance soil structure and fertility, allowing better moisture infiltration and retention in the soil. This, in turn, reduces run-off and consequent soil erosion, and improves nutrient uptake. When they avoid digging or ploughing, or reduce the use of flooding in rice production, such systems also cut GHG emissions through reducing fossil fuel use and the production of nitrous oxide and methane. They also use less water.

BOX 5
Precedent for Sustainable Food Production System of Rice Intensification (SRI)

SRI is an extraordinary example of how, by changing agronomic practices, crops can be grown more sustainably, require fewer purchased inputs, have lower demands for fresh water, and produce higher yields. Small-scale farmers like it because they make more money; some scientists don't know how to react because nobody can explain all the science behind the remarkable performance of the crop; and agricultural input companies try to shoot it down, because it harms their sales prospects.

The underlying idea is to create conditions in which rice plants can grow to express their full productive potential. This means wide spacing of very young plants, no puddling of the soil, keeping soil moisture levels up but without flooding (as, contrary to general perceptions, rice thrives in a well aerated soil), and using organic compost or manure rather than inorganic fertilizers – to "feed the soil to feed the plant". Grown in this way, rice plants develop big root systems and many tillers, and produce large heads and grains. They are also more resilient to pests and diseases, so are less dependent on pesticides than crops grown conventionally. Farmers increase yields by around 50 percent, cut seed use by 80 percent, save water (25 to 50 percent) and slash GHG methane emissions – and make more money!

The technology, originally developed in Madagascar but now taken up in over 40 countries, produces good results under all kinds of social and environmental conditions. The secret of its success lies in the way it harnesses soil biological processes and uses them to enable rice plants to express their full potential rather than grow like a bonsai[xxx].

The research that is required to come up with other similar types of innovation is likely to be of low interest to private sector investors. The implication is that the shift to greater sustainability must be underpinned by a substantial increase in publicly funded and executed agricultural research at both international and national levels. National efforts in agricultural extension must also be stepped up.

Biotechnology through gene manipulation may also play an important future role in creating crop and livestock varieties that can enhance the performance of such sustainable systems, for instance by improving drought tolerance and photosynthesis efficiency, or introducing biological nitrogen fixation capacities into non-leguminous crops. The fact that, at least in the short-term, output growth based on already known technologies, seems able to meet rising food demand, gives nations and global institutions time to put in place adequate safeguards to ensure that genetically modified organisms, when approved for release and accepted by farmers and consumers, do not pose undue risks. This would increase consumer confidence that they will not result in damage to health or the environment.

National and Global Policy Options

Putting the above approaches into action requires policy changes on the part of governments and at the international level. Most of the policy changes are self-evident from the above review of strategic options. However two particular areas in which policy adjustments are needed are discussed below.

Curbing excess consumption and waste. We have noted the need to curb over-consumption and waste of food, and to reduce the high risks of an income-induced dietary transition towards the damaging eating habits already adopted by many high-income consumers. It would, of course, be up to countries to adopt what they consider as the best ways of doing this. These could include consumer education aimed at inducing lifestyle changes, standard setting (e.g. on food labelling and packaging), codes of conduct or compacts with food processors and retailers aimed at ensuring that purchases are sourced from sustainable production systems, and differential value-added taxation on foods.

The most controversial of the above options is differential taxation. It has the advantage that it would not only provide an incentive to change eating and food wastage habits but also generate fiscal income with which to fund remedial actions both within the concerned country and possibly in other countries. It would be possible to design taxation systems to ensure that there would be no rise in the cost of staple foods for low-income consumers and to exempt sustainably produced and fair trade foods from tax-induced price rises. At the same time, governments could apply substantial taxes on *high footprint* foods, favoured by high- and middle-income consumers. In this way they would begin to internalise, within the price that buyers pay for these foods, the currently uncounted costs of environmental damage, GHG emissions, rising future public health expenditures and exploitative labour conditions in the food system. On the assumption that many such consumers will continue to eat to excess in spite of high taxes, this should generate substantial incremental revenue.

The pace at which effective policy changes are introduced will depend on the level and types of incentives given to countries to adopt them in the face of likely consumer resistance. And so we propose that international support should be provided to encourage countries to subscribe to a voluntary Global Mechanism to Cut Food Waste and Over-Consumption, built on principles similar to those of the existing Clean Development Mechanism for emissions trading. This would create a tradable quota system through which nations failing to bring average consumption progressively down to more sustainable and healthy levels, could buy entitlements to over-consume from grossly under-consuming countries. Countries that are eligible to sell entitlements would be required to invest the proceeds in measures to end hunger, improve childhood nutrition, cut future population growth and take up sustainable food production systems. The concept of this mechanism is outlined in the following box.

BOX 6
Global Mechanism to Cut Food Waste and Over-Consumption

Governments of countries concerned about over-consumption of food would set themselves annual targets for progressively bringing down average DES (i.e. after exports) and protein consumption from base-year levels towards, say, 3,000 kcal and 100 g protein per day by a given year (e.g. 2025 or 2050). They would establish a system of self-imposed penalties, to be paid by the State, related to a failure to meet these goals (e.g. $x per inhabitant per 100 kcal or 10 g protein over-run). The proceeds would be used to buy the right to over-consume from under-consuming countries (e.g. countries with over 10% of their population undernourished). These commitments would be incremental to any existing aid commitments. Recipient countries would use these funds for certified investments that would add to their efforts to reduce population growth, provide social protection for poor families, improve early childhood nutrition, support expansion of sustainable farming and fishing methods etc. Funds could be made available for budget or programme support either through bilateral or multilateral channels (e.g. UN agencies, international development banks), and would include resources to cover the costs of certifying that the money had been properly used for the intended purposes.

At the international level, voluntary guidelines would be prepared for the design and implementation of programmes for curbing over-consumption and for the use of any funds by under-consuming countries, including certification arrangements. They could also include indicative consumption reduction targets. Participating governments would declare their commitments and report periodically at the international level (for instance to the Committee on World Food Security - the CFS) on their performance vis-à-vis their self-imposed goals, and share information on successful policies and programmes. The success of the mechanism will depend very much on how ambitiously over-consuming countries set their targets. The more ambitious they are, the higher the chance of non-attainment and the larger the volume of resources to be mobilized to fight hunger. But even if less ambitious targets are set and achieved, this would still be a step in the right direction and result in health and environmental benefits.

More effective global governance systems for food. If a chicken dies of 'flu in Hong Kong, drought hits the grain-growing steppes of Russia, or a London-based hedge fund buys up 7% of the world's cocoa beans, shock waves are felt through the whole global food system. This inter-connectedness implies that, although individual communities and nations can do much by themselves to reduce hunger and adopt sustainable agricultural systems, their efforts will be all the more effective if supported by a benign global policy environment.

Paradoxically, the powers and capacities of the institutions responsible for ensuring the effective governance of the world's food and agricultural systems have been progressively eroded as globalization has created new demands upon them. The recent reforms in governance in response to the 2006-08 food price crisis appear to have been driven more by opportunism and institutional rivalry than by an objective assessment of what is needed.

When a dam is constructed, engineers examine the hydrology of the catchment area and design the structure to withstand the highest floods that are likely to occur in 100 years or even 250 years. It is difficult to predict the probability of catastrophic global food shortages, but it is vital, in designing a global governance system, to assume that they will take place and that the institutions from which it is constituted must be endowed *ex ante* with the powers needed to reduce their probability and mitigate their impact, so as to minimize loss of life. This is not a far-fetched vision, because, right now, failures in global food governance result in the perpetuation of a situation in which even a temporary rise in food prices pushes millions more people into chronic hunger, while those at the upper end of the income scale continue to eat to excess – and no institution has the power or influence to change this.

At the international level, therefore, there is a need for governments to jointly nurture the emergence of a global governance structure, based on existing institutions, that is endowed with the authority and powers to bring a lasting end to hunger and to guarantee global food safety and security in the long term. We believe that, at the very least, safeguards must be put in place to ensure that global food security is not exposed to undue risk through trading and stock-holding arrangements for food commodities and agricultural inputs that respond to corporate goals more than to the public interest of ensuring universal access to adequate food.

Whether all of what we propose happens depends ultimately on the commitment of governments and especially their willingness to subordinate their parochial national interests to the broader global good. In democratic societies, however, they will only act if they know that they have popular support for such approaches. This will require campaigning led by civil society.

Subsistence farming is important for improving nutrition.

Conservation agriculture. Sorghum Zero Tillage in an abandoned rice field of Rindiau, Mauritania (4,3 t/ha).

Chapter 6
Proposed Start-Up Actions

In this final chapter, we set out our proposals for initial actions that we believe need to be taken at national and global levels to begin to manage food better, in ways that will lead quite quickly to an end to hunger and to a lasting balance between food production and consumption.

We deliberately avoid being drawn into proposing detailed comprehensive programmes.

This is because we are convinced that the most important thing is for countries to embark quickly on a small number of key start-up actions, with the idea of building on these and broadening their scope as experience, institutional capacity and political backing, as well as international support, grow.

The methodology that we propose to apply in resolving complex problems such as hunger and poverty is similar to that proposed by the Romanian Professor Georgescu-Roegen.

BOX 7
Step by Step

Referring to Professor Georgescu-Roegen, Muhammad Yunus, founder of the Grameen Bank in Bangladesh, says [xxxi] "He taught me simple lessons that I have never forgotten about specific economic models that would help me construct the Grameen Bank. Through him, I learnt that I did not have to master economic formulae. The really important thing was to understand the underlying concepts that determine whether something will work. He taught me that things are not really as complicated as they seem. It is only our arrogance that makes us search for complicated and unnecessary responses to simple problems."

This point was taken up by Trueba in *The End of Hunger in 2025* [xxxii] "We can do much more if we structure our understanding of how to eradicate hunger and to break it down into simple problems. The systematic and joint resolution of simple problems can generate a synergy which helps us to resolve complex, multidimensional, problems such as hunger and poverty."

Actions at National Level

Ending Hunger by 2025. The best thing a country can do, when it decides to aim for hunger eradication, is to publicly declare its commitment to end hunger (indicating its willingness to be held accountable for results), setting clear and unequivocal national goals and resource allocations, outlining a strategy, and calling for all national institutions to contribute to its implementation to the best of their abilities within the scope of their own mandates. Subsequently, as confidence and institutional capacities grow, the time will come for setting up increasingly effective coordinating arrangements, approving legislation and widening programme scope and scale.

Specific start-up actions could include:

• **Nation-wide Targeted Social Protection plus Mother & Child Nutrition Programmes.** We propose that all governments of low- and middle-income countries should consider giving the highest priority to launching – or bringing quickly up to national scale – a unified social protection programme. This would be targeted at all families now suffering from hunger. Grants paid, wherever possible to women, could be set at a level aimed at bringing family food consumption up to at least the level of energy availability required for light work (120% of BMR), and higher if possible. We suggest that the beneficiaries of this programme should also eventually have access to nutrition education and to food supplements for mothers and infants. Each country should consider the most suitable approach for its situation, drawing on its own experience and that of other countries, especially neighbouring ones.

The total annual cost of a "minimalist" social protection programme, of the type that we propose as an entry point, targeted on the world's billion hungry, would start at around US$30 billion, and steadily decrease with the consequent fall in the number of hungry.

• **Improving Food Security amongst Subsistence and Landless Farmers.** We propose that, once a social protection programme is in place, priority should be given to improving the performance of subsistence farmers as this is the most direct and effective way of linking agricultural development to improved nutrition in rural communities. We suggest that governments should develop and implement specially designed extension programmes aimed at raising the capacity of all rural social protection beneficiary families to free themselves from hunger and malnutrition, largely on the basis of their own increased and diversified production, and other acquired skills. Participants could be encouraged to use part of their social protection grants as seed capital for engaging in joint participative learning processes, such as farmer field schools. The main public investment would be in training of trainers and in deploying them.

We suggest that similar adult vocational training programmes could be put in place to enable non-farming, especially urban, beneficiaries of social protection programmes to acquire other skills and thereby enhance their employability.

We envisage that these activities would eventually open the way for other community-led initiatives, aimed particularly at improving living conditions for people in rural areas. The focus would be especially on clean water supply and sanitation, access to better health care and education, and improving rural roads.

Feeding Humanity in 2050.

• Reducing Future Growth in Excessive Food Consumption.
The greatest progress in reducing future excessive food consumption would come from countries participating in the proposed Global Mechanism, but this is bound to take time to design and negotiate (see Chapter 5 and *Global Actions*, below). In the meantime, we urge countries to begin to explore how to curb the future excessive consumption and waste of food, and the conversion of food to non-food products.

The first step towards introducing a programme would normally be to establish a working group on the subject, with members drawn from a wide spectrum of disciplines – agriculture, medicine, nutrition, sociology and psychology, advertising and communications, physical education, sports and so on. The group would learn from local relevant experience and from that of other countries and sectors (e.g. in relation to smoking or alcohol consumption, obesity reduction) and prepare proposals for government, NGO and private sector action.

• **Towards Sustainable Intensification.** Work on this, too, could be boosted by actions at the international level (see *Global Actions*, below), but can initially be taken up nationally. We propose that, as a first step, all countries consider creating an expert working group to examine the extent, origins and nature of in-country environmental degradation and GHG emissions attributable to food production, trade, processing, distribution and consumption; to review successful experiences in developing more sustainable technologies, and, on that basis, prepare a strategy for combining increases in agricultural production to meet expanding demand with shifts in farming practices towards sustainable production systems. This would lead into proposals for research, extension, infrastructure and incentives aimed at bringing about the proposed technology transition.

Global Actions

Building Commitment for Hunger Eradication. We propose campaigning to raise the level of public consciousness about the hunger problem, to advocate for its eradication and to begin to induce lifestyle changes amongst middle/high income consumers. The lead for this would have to come from international and national NGOs and CSOs, as well as possibly religious organizations and other elements of civil society, committed to hunger eradication, better nutrition, sustainable development and human rights. The campaign could be based on an amalgamation of the on-going or planned campaigns of like-minded organizations, in view of the much greater impact potential of united rather than fragmented actions when campaigning is intended to induce changes in policies rather than to raise money for specific causes.

Towards a Long-Term Equilibrium Between Food Consumption and Supply.
• **Curbing Excessive Demand.** As noted earlier we are proposing that governments in countries facing problems of excessive food consumption and waste should adopt policies that would lead to a progressive rise in the prices of food with high environmental footprints as a result of differential taxation levels and other measures. Our proposal for the creation of a Global Mechanism (Chapter 5) is very far-reaching and warrants thorough examination before being formally proposed for adoption. We recommend that the High-Level Panel of Experts be commissioned by the Committee on World Food Security (CFS) to examine the Global Mechanism proposals and the feasibility of adopting them..

• **Sustainable Intensification.** Although many of the research centres of the Consultative Group for International Agricultural Research (CGIAR) have programmes on sustainable agriculture, livestock and fisheries, there is as yet no system-wide programme on the subject. We would like to see the Commission on Sustainable Agriculture and Climate Change, created by the CGIAR in March 2011, propose the creation of a

"Challenge Programme on Feeding the World in 2050: Research to Underpin the Shift to Sustainable Farming Systems". Such a programme, in which most CGIAR centres would take part, would address issues related to both social and environmental sustainability, as well as to climate change, and would focus strongly on supporting adaptive research by small-scale farmers, with a major focus on agro-ecological approaches to intensification. The main justification for putting additional public funding into this research is that many of the technologies that offer potentially higher levels of sustainability depend on less use of purchased inputs and are, therefore, of low interest to the private sector, although some could be addressed through public-private partnerships.

Effective Global Food Governance Systems.
We see a need for the creation of an Independent Commission of Enquiry to review the mandates and recent performance of the institutions – both public and private – that are now collectively responsible for the global governance of the agri-food system and, on the basis of this assessment, determine their capability to manage potentially much more serious future food crises in ways that minimize loss of life and livelihoods. The Commission would make recommendations for a suitable structure and for the powers that should be given to its component elements. The United Nations Human Rights Council might be the appropriate body to convene this Commission.

Harness New Sources of Financial and Technical Cooperation.
We recommend that, as an extension of the review of the proposed "Global Mechanism", the CFS also take the lead in exploring how obligatory compensatory transfers, especially those related to reducing GHG emissions and changing food consumption behaviour, could become increasingly substantial

and predictable sources of finance for investments required for shifting to sustainable food consumption and production systems. These mechanisms could eventually substitute for less dependable bilateral aid.

We also propose that FAO widen its activities for facilitating a much expanded programme of South-South Cooperation between developing countries, including support for both bilateral and trilateral agreements under which richer countries finance the provision of services provided by developing countries.

What You Can Do

Ultimately, progress towards a hunger-free world depends on the actions of individuals, whether farmers who decide to change the ways in which they manage their crops and livestock, or consumers who may deliberately choose to pay for the full cost of their food, for instance through purchasing fair trade goods that are ethically and sustainably sourced. Some readers, especially those involved in campaigning or policy making, may be able to apply some of our ideas in their work.

We expect, however, that many of you who are reading this are consumers living in developed countries, or in the cities of developing countries. If this is the case, we suggest that you consider changing your lifestyle in order to cut food waste and over-consumption. The most practical way of making a difference is to change your shopping and cooking habits so as to eliminate food waste, and to adjust your family eating habits towards foods that, while providing adequate nutrition, have low ecological footprints. If enough people do this, it will reduce pressure on the expansion of the agricultural frontier and help to cut greenhouse gas emissions. The potential health dividend is also large.

Beyond this, the best you can do is to help awaken your friends and neighbours to the scale of the hunger problem, to its human impact, and especially to the relative ease with which it can be resolved. Please support civil society organizations that are campaigning for the same approaches. As knowledge of the issue is broadened, this can lead to a stronger constituency of support for action by governments.

If you are really convinced by what you have read, then you can start to get brave! **Please sign up your support to the One Billion Hungry Project through our website** www.endofhunger2025.com, **register your personal commitment and share your thoughts**. See who else has also signed up, and decide what you will do together to end hunger by 2025, and to accelerate the shift to more sustainable farming systems. Spread the word through your social networks or websites. Make things actually happen! These are the great challenges facing our generation, and our future credibility hangs on how effective we are in getting action taken.

My Commitments

I commit myself to work actively towards the eradication
of hunger and to engage people
I know in this endeavour,
putting pressure on governments to take action.

I commit myself to change my shopping and eating habits
in order to contribute to greater sustainability
in the use of natural resources.

I commit myself to avoid wastage and extravagant use
of food, whose production consumes water, energy and
hard work and, in addition, contributes to climate change.

Notes

References to WP relate to Working Papers by the named author, available on the companion website **www.endofhunger2025.com**.

These Notes are also available on the website to facilitate electronic access to sources.

I   FAO (2011) *Global Food Losses and Food Waste*, Rome,.
www.fao.org/fileadmin/user_upload/ags/publications/GFL_web.pdf

II   www.fao.org/righttofood/common/ecg/51635_en_General_Comment_No.12.pdf

III   Sen, Amartya, *Poverty and Famines: An Essay on Entitlement and Deprivation*, Oxford, 1981.

IV   See: FAO (2002) *World Agriculture; towards 2015/2030, Summary Report*, Rome.

V   FAO (2009) *State of Food Insecurity in the World*
ftp://ftp.fao.org/docrep/fao/012/i0876e/i0876e.pdf

VI   See: FAO (2007) *Human Energy Requirements*, Rome.
www.fao.org/docrep/007/y5686e/y5686e01.htm#TopOfPage

[VII]   FAO (2008) *State of Food Insecurity in the World*
ftp://ftp.fao.org/docrep/fao/011/i0291e/i0291e00.pdf

[VIII]   See World Food Programme (WFP) website
www.wfp.org/hunger/malnutrition

[IX]   For these and other figures relating to the number of hungry people, see:
FAO (2010) *State of Food Insecurity in the World,* Rome.
www.fao.org/docrep/013/i1683e/i1683e.pdf

[X]   FAO Food Price Index (monthly),
www.fao.org/worldfoodsituation/wfs-home/foodpricesindex/en/

[XI]   See Hawkes, C. and Murphy, S., An Overview of Global Food Trade.
(Chap. 2 of Hawkes, C. *et al. Trade, Food, Diet and Health: Perspectives
and Policy Options*, Wiley-Blackwell, 2009).

[XII]   For these and other related figures on population, see UN (2010)
Revision of World Population, New York.

[XIII]   The term was first coined by Sydney Afriat, who has recently written a
short treatise on *What happened to the population problem? – and other
questions*, Bright Pen, 2010.
www.authorsonline.co.uk

[XIV]   MacMillan, Andrew, WP 2

[XV]   Graziano da Silva, José, WP

[XVI]   For a lot of facts and figures about energy use and greenhouse gas
emissions, see Pitman, Walter, Lectures on Energy and Public Policy,
Columbia University, 2003
www.ldeo.columbia.edu/edu/dees/U4735/lectures/09.html

[XVII] For a good summary of land and water resource availability, see FAO (2002) *World Agriculture: towards 2015/2030. Summary Report*, Rome. ftp://ftp.fao.org/docrep/fao/004/y3557e/y3557e.pdf

[XVIII] European Nitrogen Assessment www.nine-esf.org/node/204

[XIX] Committee on World Food Security, High-Level Panel of Experts on Food Security and Nutrition, *Report on Price Volatility* – A Zero Draft Consultation Paper, May 2011 http://typo3.fao.org/fileadmin/user_upload/fsn/docs/HLPE/HLPE_Study_on_price_volatility_-_V0_draft_May.pdf

[XX] www.fao.org/worldfoodsituation/wfs-home/foodpricesindex/en/

[XXI] http://siteresources.worldbank.org/INTPROSPECTS/Resources/334934-1110315015165/Migration&DevelopmentBrief10.pdf

[XXII] See FAO, IFAD, IEED publication www.ifad.org/pub/land/land_grab.pdf

[XXIII] For a wide-ranging discussion on this issue, see Kent, George (ed), *Global Obligations for the Right to Food*, New York, 2008.

[XXIV] For detailed figures, see MacMillan, Andrew, WP 3

[XXV] A similar conclusion is reached in INRA & CIRAD (2009) *Agrimonde: scenarios and challenges for feeding the World in 2050*, Montpellier

[XXVI] See FAO (2011) *Save and Grow: A policymakers' guide to the sustainable intensification of smallholder crop production*, Rome www.fao.org/ag/save-and-grow/index_en.html

[xxvii] Tutu, Desmond, *Hunger Can be Solved* (op-ed), quoted at www.oxfam.org.nz/newsroom.asp?action=view&type=News&id=2816

[xxviii] See FAO (2000) *State of Food Insecurity in the World*, Rome. www.fao.org/FOCUS/E/SOFI00/img/sofirep-e.pdf

[xxix] Many documents on FFS in all continents are available at www.farmerfieldschool.info/

[xxx] *Paddy and Water Environment*, Vol 9, Issue 1.

[xxxi] Counts, Alex. *Small Loans, Big Dreams – How Nobel Prize Winner Muhammad Yunus and Microfinance Changed the World*, Wiley, 2008.

[xxxii] Trueba, Ignacio, *El Fin del hambre en 2025 – Un desafío para nuestra generación*, Madrid, 2006.

Acronyms

BMR: Basic Metabolic Rate

CFS: Committee on World Food Security

CGIAR: Consultative Group for International Agricultural Research

CSO: Civil Society Organization

DES: Dietary Energy Supply

FAO: Food and Agriculture Organization of the United Nations

FFS: Farmer Field Schools

CHG: Greenhouse Gas

HLPE: High-Level Panel of Experts (of the CFS)

NGO: Non-Governmental Organization

SRI: System of Rice Intensification

UPM: Technical University of Madrid

WFP: World Food Programme

WWII: Second World War